Travel to Live

A proven path from upheaval & uncertainty to living the life you dream

An Inspirational True Story
By Sue Robson

Travel to Live

© 2018 Sue Robson. All rights reserved.

No part of this publication may be reproduced, distributed or transmitted, in any form or by any means, including photocopying, recording, or other electronic or mechanical methods, without the prior written permission of the publisher, except in the case of brief quotations, embodied in reviews and certain other non-commercial use is permitted by copyright law.

Published by Miss Sue H Robson

ISBN (Kindle) 978-0-9876355-0-1
ISBN (paperback, colour) 978-0-9876355-2-5

Photo Credits: Sue Robson

Editing by Lizette Balsdon
www.editingqueen.co.za

Cover Design by Christos Angelidakis
angelidakis.chris@gmail.com
Instagram: @bookcovers_by_chris

Interior Formatting by Kim Carr
http://kimsonthemark.com

Dedication

I dedicate this book to my family who inspire me on many levels.

To my grandmother for her wisdom, and to my mother for her unconditional love and support. To my sister for being there for me, as my best friend. To my father for showing me the value of the dollar. Dad had the pleasure out of making some of our toys in our younger days, in place of buying everything.

This is what I am dedicated to:

When writing the STORY of your life, don't let anyone else HOLD the pen.

Do not edit your life story while it's still unravelling.

Value the power of the written word.

Patience is a virtue; it is better to simply wait and allow rather than to force.

Embrace my family for they are the roots of my being.

Be brave, stand up for my authenticity, graciously.

Believe "Who I am is enough".

GRAB YOUR FREE GIFT!

IDENTIFY & CLARIFY

MINI CAREER SUCCESS JOURNAL

To get the best experience with this book, download the Identify & Clarify Workbook to keep track of all your thoughts, visions and ideas in your own personal journal.

You can access that here for free:
https://www.suehelenrobson.com/ttl7dayplan

Contents

Chapter One: Why Did I Write This Book?	1
Chapter Two: Introduction	5
Chapter Three: Career Path	14
Chapter Four: My Career in Luxury Super Yachts	27
Chapter Five: My Travel Destinations	37
Chapter Six: Dreams Really Do Come True	56
Chapter Seven: References	67
Acknowledgements	70
Identify & Clarify Mini Career Success Journal	73
A Final Note to the Reader	74

Chapter One
Why Did I Write This Book?

I MADE A COMMITMENT to myself to live the life I dream and let the Gypsy in me roam freely in many directions.

My grandmother has been the biggest inspiration in my life. My love for my grandmother is strong. She was a spiritual woman, who never really took it into the world. She often saw ghosts and had conversations with them; at times, she drew them in some of her sketches. In her other sketches, she enjoyed sketching interesting people. She sent her sketch to the Fred Hollows foundation; they loved it and there it is filed.

One example of a person she drew was
Dr Fred Hollows of the Fred Hollows Foundation.

Fred got things done. He always pushed for change and, because of that, put in motion a legacy to end avoidable blindness. In his time as a humanitarian and eye surgeon, Fred helped restore eyesight to thousands of people in Australia and overseas.

He was an amazing eye doctor who travelled the world, helping those less fortunate.

The detail in Gran's sketches made them look authentic. I believe that is because her subject inspired her.

We often shared our ghost stories—this was natural for us—and we would laugh at what other people would think of us if we told them our experiences. This is what made our relationship so special, for I often had ghosts visit me in different places around the world.

She loved listening to classical music for her afternoon meditation. Early on in her life she sang. She loved opera and joined a musical society group so she could sing and act and it made her feel alive. I often heard her singing to herself around the home. She loved the feeling of her voice resonating through her body; she said it lit her up inside.

Highly intuitive, she was my guardian angel, especially while I was traveling. I would Skype call her from various destinations around the globe and we would chat for hours. She lived with my Auntie—*well,* my grandmother was a very independent woman and she made sure she was not a burden. She insisted on having her own granny flat built on one wing of my auntie's home.

When I called they would open the atlas on the dining table and look to see where I was in the world, as we spoke. My aunt and Gran would leave the atlas on the table and look at it often; they said it made them feel as though they were a part of my journey as I travelled the globe. My grandmother loved travel; however she did not travel until she was in her sixties—another amazing thing about her. She created journals of her travels with the postcards she collected.

I would call her as often as I could, especially if I had questions and needed directions to the challenges that lay ahead for me.

I would ask her and she would share her visions. She would enlighten me with some amazing insights that supported me in making the right choices that aligned with my highest good—this was vital during my time away from home.

My grandmother was a remarkable woman with so many gifts; it's a real shame she never shared her story. She passed away at the age of ninety-seven, but she's still with me today in my heart and thoughts. I know she is here with me writing this book.

During my meditations and creative journaling it, I was often told I am a lightworker. I didn't really know what that actually meant in reality, especially in the early days of this path I was paving out. The more I walked along this path, the more confident I became in trusting in the unknown.

It is upon writing this book that I have come to an understanding of what being a lightworker truly means. For me, I need to honour all the things I said I would do; to walk my talk, which meant I must lead by example. Yet more importantly, I needed to talk, for I was certainly doing the walk.

I needed to follow on from where my grandmother left off and share my story. In time, I will share hers to, for she truly was a remarkable woman with many special gifts. I know she wanted the world to know about this, but with fear, stinking thinking, and self-doubt in mind, she never did.

As the storyteller of my first book, I am dedicated to *talk my walk*, to follow on where my grandmother left off, and to let the world know who I am.

My intention is to spark the fire in you to follow your dreams wherever they may lead. To be the storyteller of your life and let the world know who you are. Take the risk of looking like a fool, acting reckless in the desire to follow your dream, and live the adventure of being alive.

> *"Don't just be successful; be a legend."*
> *- Stevie Nicks*

This quote sparked the fire in my belly. I read it shortly after my grandmother's passing. I strongly remember feeling her yearning to be seen in the world. I am coming into the realisation of needing to talk my walk. Those words ignite my passion even more now, to follow my dream and write my story. It is time for me to be brave, honour my authenticity, and share this with the world.

I realise I don't have to be Stevie Nicks to be a legend. I simply have to believe that who I am is enough.

Chapter Two

Introduction

As this book is about finding my ultimate vocation, I have written it in a *playful* CV format. Editing, updating, and changing my CV to suit different roles was a constant. I must have written hundreds during my search for the ultimate vocation.

Let me clarify, for me vocation is not just about finding a job. It is about finding a lifestyle that makes my heart sing, where my mind can express itself creatively, and my body can dance wild and carefree in many directions. I am committed to live the life I dream of. My goal is to have the freedom to be in charge of my schedule and my lifestyle. For me, this is a truly blessed life.

Hello: My name is *Miss Sue Robson*.

I am: *a woman* who has never had children, nor have I been married at the time of writing this book.

My motto: is to see all points of view, *but* to have a conviction in my own.

Born: Sydney, New South Wales, December 1965

Passport: Australian—an open ticket to travel the globe

Visa: B1/B2—I highly recommend it

Website: www.suehelenrobson.com

Lives: in many places. At the time of writing this, I am with family on the Gold Coast.

Sun Sign: Capricorn

Capricorn: Astrological signs give you greater knowledge of who you are.

Capricorn, being the tenth sign of the zodiac, is all about hard work. Those born under this sign are more than happy to put in a full day, realising that it will likely take many those days to reach the top. That's no problem, since Capricorns are both ambitious and determined. They know they will get there.

Life is one big project for these folks; *for me it is a creative project due to other factors playing out in my Natal Chart.* They adapt to this by adopting a businesslike approach to most everything they do.

Capricorns are practical as well, taking things one step at a time and being as realistic and pragmatic as possible. However, there were times I was unconventional in my approach to things; nonetheless, the core essence of the practical part of me is what helped me achieve the results. Having this knowledge supports me to better understand, as a Capricorn, that I am extremely dedicated to my goals, almost to the point of stubbornness. Those victories sure smell sweet, though, and that thought alone will keep Capricorns going.

Education

I completed the end of school without a certificate to validate my education. *Guess I don't need one?* At school, I was not very good at colouring inside the lines, anyway. As it turns out, this has set a platform for a life that reflects the same. Living outside the lines sheds light on a life created out of upheaval, uncertainty, and unfamiliarity.

Travel is my vehicle; the world is my playground; adventure is my teacher; and ambition is my driving force.

My determination to grow spiritually, personally and professionally took me on a journey of self-discovery. I am dedicated to my goals, which on my journey to find a suitable vocation, were somewhat unconventional. I recognised that racking up achievements wasn't going to fulfil my ambitious nature. I came to realise that I needed to trust my intuition and follow that lead wherever it led me. *Go on curiosity; take that risk with unwavering faith. It will all be ok,* I say to myself. Turns out life itself became my educational platform and these experiences have become my skill set.

Skill Set

Adapting to any environment came naturally to me; I started doing this at age of seventeen.

As a visionary, I see adversity as an opportunity to make a choice, when the situation or environment changes dynamically. I learnt to see all points of view, *but* quickly learnt to know what was mine. I needed a firm sense of self beyond how others perceived me.

It took courage and time to grow into these skills. Over time, survival taught me to *STOP and* listen to the quiet voice inside, feel what my gut instincts were showing me, wait for guidance, and—when the time was right—onward I would go. During these times, the place of uncertainty looked clearer than staying in the outmoded. I was a curious soul on a mission to find my ultimate vocation, and so it felt natural for me to step into the unknown.

"After all, therein lies the adventure..."

Hobbies and Interests

A few things happened early in my life, prompting me to question myself.

Who am I? Where do I belong?

I wanted to find the answer to my questions. Being somewhat naïve, I knew I needed a tangible tool. My creative nature wanted this to be playful and fun.

Creative writing—free flowing through my pencils—gave me a place to express my feelings, thoughts, and emotions safely without judgement or criticism from myself, as I dived into a journey of self-discovery. My studies of Spiritual Astrology gave clarity to my inner workings more easily. I have written hundreds of journals and continue to enjoy this practice today.

I studied Spiritual Astrology with Ashtara at her property on the Gold Coast Hinterland. For me, Astrology is likened to the blueprint of your soul. Every planet has a place in each chakra, which correlates to various organs within that part of the body.

I started building my awareness and confidence with small elements which occurred in my daily life—for example, a pinched sciatic nerve, lower back pain, bloated abdomen, hay fever—just to mention a few. I could relate each ailment to that part of my body which correlated to that particular chakra. As the external planets transit, they would send beams of light to my soul, exposing the unconscious memory of the emotional wounding via the ailment I was experiencing. This indicated what I needed to look at, so I could learn from it. This supported me in understanding that I can change my external world via my internal world.

Coming onto completion of my studies with Ashtara, I was led to another teacher, Leyolah. a teacher of Kundalini Dance. This is a sacred practice through the chakra system, which works with body movement, breath, and music. I love music and often find inspiration in the lyrics. In the dance, I can be free from thoughts as I close my eyes and let my body move to the music. Fascinated by Leyolah and her teachings, I was one of the first groups of students to go through her first training program to become a facilitator of Kundalini Dance. This dance practice enabled me to dance freely, using the breath technique that works best in each chakra, whilst listening to the appropriate music. This simply allowed my body to remove stuck, stale, stagnant, and negative energy from my being without judgement, criticism, or over analysing—just simply by dancing in this way.

Astrology and Dance are powerful tools in the Art of Healing.

I would like to bring clarity to my Hobbies and Interests, with the intention to show you the Healing Arts I studied are not hocus pocus; they are genuine tools to support you in your life.

Astrology and Dance are Powerful Tools in the Art of Healing

Because I enjoy writing creatively, I thought it was time to test my skills as a writer and entered a competition. What inspired me to enter is the subject; "Write a short story, about yourself or someone who has gone through a Health Crisis".

However, my story is not based on the experience of a physical illness; rather it is a journey inwards of self-discovery.

I have studied Astrology for several years as a hobby. I joined a small group and we gathered each week for four years in an inspiring and beautiful cottage in the hinterland of the Gold Coast.

Our teacher, Ashtara, who was in her fifties, then, was an amazing lady. Her teachings came from her personal experiences. Ashtara's methods are unique and unusual. We covered Spiritual, Medical, and Esoteric Astrology. She taught us beyond the mathematics and science. It is best to integrate this information into your daily life, and she showed us how.

My passion is Medical Astrology. Astrology is linked to the blueprint of the soul. Therefore, every planet has a place in each chakra, which correlates to various organs within that part of the body.

I started building my awareness and confidence with small ailments that occurred in my daily life, for example my pinched sciatica nerve, lower back pain, bloated abdomen and cramping leg muscles, to name a few. As the external planets transit, they send beams of light to my soul, exposing the unconscious memory of the emotional wounding via the ailment I am experiencing. This indicated what I needed to look at and learn from, in order to change my external world via my internal world.

As these ailments occurred to show me what I needed to look at—a series of unexpected events came up simultaneously, shapeshifting my life. Briefly, I had moved from Sydney to the Gold Coast, ended my second relationship, and started a new business. I was in debt, lost my driver's license, sold my car, and moved into a two-bedroom cottage on my own.

INTRODUCTION

In the beginning of my studies, with all that was occurring, I experienced self-sacrificial behavioural patterns and could feel a deep transformation occurring within. Pluto rules transformation and a need to let go of the darkness within. Saturn on the other hand, brings forth our deepest fears to be cleaned and healed. What an intense emotional journey I experienced—a frightening time indeed.

Honestly, I am glad I lived alone so I could process this without over analysing. *Just keep writing everything down*, I said to myself. *It will all make sense soon.* Those weekly classes were my saving grace during this difficult time.

I set up my second bedroom up as a teaching room for selected clients and friends, to build confidence in my physic abilities and to trust my skills as a healer and teacher. I had some incredible healing sessions with others and myself. During my meditations, I would delve deeply into myself to uncover my skills, talents, and abilities in the healing realm. I wanted to become clearer and more conscious.

I meditated on a full moon in Scorpio when something amazing happened! I had opened up what felt like a volcano that had been lying dormant for a long time. Something huge had erupted!

Over the next two years, I experienced a total clearing out of old, outmoded beliefs. All limiting, restricting, and destructive beliefs flooded my mind and emotions. I was shown—through Astrology—where these had stemmed from, what area of my life they related to, and why I created these beliefs.

At times, the intensity of these memories, emotions, and visions overwhelmed me. I felt so alone, at times—it was frightening. Physically, I wasn't ill; my healing was internal. Parts of me were dying and I was grieving! My life became chaotic, as I was changing within. All I had learnt was now being tested.

The insight of Astrology supported me in a greater understanding. As the series of events occurred, I would relate this back to my natal chart. I wrote every thought, feeling, vision, ailment, and experience down. I have written many journals.

For example, transiting Venus sent beams of light to my soul, exposing my lower back pain. My thoughts were revealed.

I did not feel financially supported. I was allowing money problems to worry me, as my negative thoughts were on *lack* of money. Mind you, my business was doing well. The underlying belief and emotional wounding revolved around the fact that I did not value my ideas or myself. Note at this time, I was struggling financially due to a debt from a prior experience, before going into business.

My unconscious patterns, rooted deep inside me, had me believe I was not good enough to earn my own money and support myself. How could I possibly earn enough money to meet my needs by doing what I love to do?

This supported the belief (subconsciously) that I wasn't good enough.

I was constantly told by my teachers and in my school reports that I was not trying hard enough. "You can do better", "That is not good enough", "Sue, stop disrupting the class".

I was always in trouble for not doing as I was told. I remember how mad that made me feel as a child. I remember feeling confused as to how I was misunderstood; this isolated me. The loneliness I felt at the time, made me sad.

These experiences do not go away; they are buried deep inside. Believe me, they are still there waiting to come out in some way.

Ideally, find a method for you to release these toxic emotional wounds from inside you. For me, Astrology and Kundalini

Dance works well; it feeds my mind with the Art and Science of Astrology, and the Dance practice shifts stuck energy. Without the mind—simply body movement—music and breath work will free you up on all levels.

My passion for Astrology and Kundalini Dance with their healing qualities is a conscious part of my daily life. In time, I will write a book and share more detail of what I have learned and how these tangible tools supported me. I have come to understand and appreciate what it is to "be your own best friend".

Turns out I came third in the contest. Upon reading the first two stories, it is no wonder they received those placements.

As I shapeshift myself, my life reflects this and from there, everyone benefits, my family, friends, people I work with and even strangers, it is a ripple effect.

Chapter Three
Career Path

A Major turning point

A FEW UNEXPECTED EVENTS happened here that shaped my life and me.

I will only touch briefly on this here, so you have an idea what shaped me.

Firstly as a family we moved from New South Wales to Queensland. *Yikes!*

Shortly after that, my parents separated, Dad staying in Queensland and Mum moving back to Sydney, New South Wales—*crikey!*

Everything I knew, all my friends, my wonderful childhood now drastically changed.

Life as I knew it was now uprooted for good.

To add to this unfoldment, I only had three months left of my Year Ten schooling to complete, in which we were told Queensland would validate my school certificate, *it turned out that was not the case*, so I finished school with no certificate to validate my education in school.

Oh well, guess I don't need one?

The memories of my carefree childhood are rich in the simplicity of living in harmony with nature. We grew up living opposite an abundant rainforest. This connection to nature in all its magnificence was my playground. This is what encouraged me to live the life I dreamed and to let the Gypsy in me live freely in many directions.

Why not? I was never good at staying inside the lines, anyway.

Living outside the lines

Living outside the lines sheds light on a life created out of upheaval, uncertainty, and unfamiliarity. At school I was not very good at colouring inside the lines and as it turns out, that has set a platform for a life that reflects the same.

I spent the next couple of years floundering around wondering what to do with my life. Questioning everything in my world and inside of me. Everything was uncertain and I felt very unsettled. I wondered where I belonged, what is this all about. Why was this put in the equation, when everything was going so well? It was tough for all of us. My sister was finishing school in a new school and environment she did not enjoy, and both my parents were finding their new footing as well.

Just before my eighteenth birthday, I decided it was time to find a place where I can be independent. However, having no certificate or any real hands on job experience, made it a bit difficult.

Briefly working with my Natal chart will give you an idea of how Astrology works in your life and inside of yourself. I have Moon in Aries; Aries is about being independent and adventurous. I had done this in many lives before. The moon here is past lives, but as it was on my descendant, that is the learning curve to find balance, in and outside of self. There were quite a few lessons I needed to learn. Aries can tend to be impulsive or spontaneous; it delivers very different results. I think, in the early days of having my life up rooted, it was vital that I learnt to understand the difference and find a balance between impulsive and spontaneous. Over time, I worked on that part of myself, as I did not want to have that feeling of not knowing where I belonged or what the heck was I doing again. As the saying goes, I felt like a fish out of water, flapping around.

I saw an advertisement in the newspaper for a housekeeper position on Great Keppel Island. I thought that, with my lack of skill set right now, this surely is a job I could do. I posted a letter, and shortly after, I received the phone call of my enquiry to work on Great Keppel Island in the Whitsundays—wow!—and working on an island; how exciting!

That is how we did things in those days; technology was not as advanced as it is today.

The unsettled part of me knew I needed more than just a job at this early stage of my life. Working and living the Island, life serves me on many levels as I would have accommodation, food, a community; my basic needs are met. I could create friendships, and I had a job in which I could gain some experience and earn an income. For me, at this time in my life, it was a wonderful answer to the situation I was in.

CAREER PATH

Working on Great Keppel Island in the 80s was fun; as we are still in the hippie era. Everyone had their unique way of making their room feel like home. Sarongs were draped on the windows, candles and incense burned in coloured bowls on makeshift tables, created with milk crates turned upside down; brought to life with a bit of timber and of course a sarong or fabric placed over the top. A creative space and time, we made mobile hangings out of dried wood and shells we collected on the beach.

The freshly-picked flowers, different shaped pebbles, and rocks I found on my walks, made great decorations on the shelves, where I placed my favourite books and music. The atmosphere in the staff area filled with music being playing from each room. Some folk would sit on the veranda, playing guitars and singing. I felt carefree living the hippie life on the island; the gypsy in me loved this environment.

A year has passed and a few of the folk I made friends with were onto the next thing; they asked me to join them. Free will to the wild at heart ran through me like a summer breeze, whispering sweet messages to follow your heart wherever it may lead you. "Of course, I would love to join you," I said. For me it is another adventure, *why wouldn't I say yes? There is no question there from me! Let's go.*

I travelled around, exploring the region for the next few years.

A little later on, an opportunity to work as a hostess in a Meet and Greet role on Lindeman Island was advertised in the paper. I thought that could be a fun role.

"Yes, why not?" I said to myself. I enjoyed Island life already— it is a good fit! I applied with a letter and received a phone call shortly after. Staying with a friend who had a landline made this opportunity easy, as no one I knew had a mobile phone in that day.

Lindeman Island was a bit more modern in a sense, but as the staff area is in the old part, the ambience of that hippie era was easily created. The gypsy in me found it easy to decorate this space into a home, remembering what I learnt on Great Keppel. I used the shells and sticks I collected to make mobiles; the rocks and flowers I found on my walks, filled the shelves; and the coloured bowls I bought while exploring the region were filled with sand from the beach—perfect for candles. They were placed on the tables we made from milk crates; just add a bit of timber, throw a sarong over, and you have a table.

I hung my pictures from the adventures I shared with friends on the wall; after all the Whitsundays is my playground. I loved Whitehaven beach and some of the more remote islands we ventured to; it was picturesque. I felt so carefree here. There was nothing to distract you from being close to nature in all its raw and natural beauty. It felt like home; the lifestyle was similar to the childhood I enjoyed playing till dark, in the rainforest across the road. Back in those days, most of the Islands were Australian-owned; it was a laid back time.

Townsville Breakwater Casino was my next place of employment. It was an exciting time in Townsville and Queensland. This is the first time to have approval for and to build a Casino in Queensland. This was a big step forward in 1984.

Due to this, there was plenty of work available at the *new* Breakwater Casino. I saw a suitable position advertised, for a hostess. I felt confident with my recent experience as Hostess on Lindeman Island, so I applied with a letter. Turns out, my recent experience in a similar role was a blessing when I received the call to come in for an interview. The role advertised was for a Hostess in the Piano Lounge Bar. At the interview, my vibrant and enthusiastic personality shone brightly. This supported me in being hired, yeah!

At this time, there was one allocated for South Queensland and this one here in North Queensland.

The State has resolved to permit the establishment and operation of casinos in the State of Queensland by licensing one casino facility in Northern Queensland and one in Southern Queensland.

It was exciting to be a part of this. The Breakwater Casino was always busy; there were visitors from everywhere, who wanted to be a part of the excitement and hype.

The Hotel and Casino was top notch—full class, all the bells and whistles, a high end establishment indeed. It was a prosperous time for all the high rollers, to come and state their importance.

Career development was easy with an abundance of work available. Staff could take advantage of these opportunities, and cross train in all departments. It was exciting for those who wanted to advance their education, experience, and skills.

Living a land-based lifestyle took a bit of getting used to. Money was going out like never before. There was rent, utility bills, transport, food, and clothes. Yikes, does this mean I have to tighten my budget? *Absolutely not*, there is socialising to be had! You could always find someone you knew at the local bars; after all, this is the fun part—making new friends opened doors for adventure.

Finding a place to live was easy with the help of the hotel's human resources department. There are so many people who have come here to find work. They set up groups of people, and we would come together to get to know each other, and then see who would be a good fit to share with. It was fun; if one didn't work out, another did. Easy times were here.

This is how I handled the unexpected and turned it into a fulfilling experience. Born with my sun in Capricorn, it was natural for me to be pragmatic or practical. I learnt to live in the real world, by wearing comfortable shoes. Even though

I lived a rather unconventional lifestyle, I was forming a relationship with the gypsy in me and the practical nature of my being.

Who knew the story of a stranger could change the way you view your life? It has mine.

Who knows? Maybe by the end of this book you may, too.

The best years of my life

I was twenty, and it was time to head back home to Sydney, New South Wales. It felt right, as Mum has bought a home, and my sister has moved back. Mum has given us a place to call home; so together, we started a new chapter of our life.

Living with mum and sister, being grounded and creating foundations was a really exciting time. Actually, those were the best years of my life. If I could turn back time, this would be a highlight for me.

Our home was an open door and all the friends we grew up with came flooding back into our life and our home. Everyone loved coming to "Robbo's Home", as children we nicknamed everything and everyone.

A few examples—My sister's nickname came from a friend who lives on a farm with a cat called Carpussa. At night, the cat would go on the prowl (like cats do) and at that stage in our life; we were all out and about at night socialising. We joked around teasing my sister, as she was the youngest, saying she was on the prowl—truth is, all of us were. I feel we all had a bit of Capussa in us.

My girlfriend would say, "Sue, you make me dizzy, Miss Lizzy", as I was full of ideas and visions. I loved adventures, to explore new places, go on road trips, despite the fact that I was working days, nights, and hours all over the place.

Over time, it broke down to Lizard. Turns out the symbol Lizard is the dreamer of the dream. For me, it is the messages dreams bring to me in the night. Curious to decipher their meaning, I would keep a dream journal. A part of me already loved to write; it was easy to enjoy this daily practice. My curiosity of the hidden workings of this mysterious Universe could be brought to light in my dream journals.

Ironically enough, these nicknames highlighted things about myself I may not have seen otherwise. Even if it was a bit of fun, it did make sense.

Not long after we settled as a family—just the three of us—I found a job at the local hotel, which was the hub for social networking and community. It was a large hotel with several areas to it. The hotel reminded me of the Breakwater Casino—only without the casino, or bells and whistles.

I enjoyed working across all areas of the hotel incorporating the public bar, lounge bar, Sunday sessions with live music, the nightclub, and Jazz club. I saw some great musicians here, including Monica and the Moochers, and James Morrison. This Jazz Club was opened a few nights a week. I worked everything—days, nights, shift work, weekends -it was a great opportunity to expand my skill set and gain valuable knowledge.

There was a part of me *(North Node is the Souls destiny in Astrology)* that was used to learning, taking in new information, and getting a handle on it quickly. It was fun; it fed my soul.

In my Natal Chart, I have Jupiter and North Node in Gemini in the 9th House of travel and higher learning. Taking in vast amounts of information and processing this is natural for me. Opposite Mercury and South Node in Sagittarius, is the third house of communication. I love writing; free writing my thoughts, ideas, emotions, and experiences down on paper taught me to understand what is mine and what is another's. A writing practice I work with today.

It was a very social time. I met my first boyfriend—then my second boyfriend—during this period. I was grounded, had my roots down, had many beautiful friends, and a real sense of belonging. It was a good time in my life.

Days off were filled with adventures, camping in different locations, water skiing, horse riding, and just enjoying life in the outdoors. Life in the eighties in Australia was a safe time to explore. We partied at night in Kings Cross and the Inner City, into the wee hours without need to concern for our safety.

To note—Kings Cross in the early 90s, was known for its mile-long nightclub <u>red light district</u>. Called the "Golden Mile".

Business in the 90s

As a family, the three of us—mum, sister and I—decided to pack up and move to the Gold Coast, Queensland, where mum's sister had recently moved. Upon moving to Queensland, I caught up with a friend that I haven't seen for a long time. I saw this as an act of fate, for she was working in her family business and suggested I do a course and see what I think. Well, I never looked back.

The Business Capricorn in me was ready and *more* than pleased to start my own business. It is in the nail industry, which provided me with a fulfilling profession for ten years. Working alongside my sister made it an enjoyable journey.

Taking the reins of my life, working for myself, running my own show, meant that I could be in charge of my schedule and my life.

My sister had set up a hair salon; it is here that I joined her. Mum had a part of this too; we are a close family, and this is what we did.

I was able to work my nail business under the same roof, so it was a good fit. It was a very social time for us, getting out there, promoting our business as a sister-family combo; we were warmly embraced by the community.

The 90s on the Gold Coast was a perfect time as many opportunities to talk our business flourished. Main Beach and Marina Mirage were alive; you were bound to run into someone you knew. There were balls, charity events, and the bars—or *"watering holes"*—were filled with young guns doing the same. During this time, each of our business was doing well. I wanted to buy my first home and I did so with mum. We were putting foundations down again. My sister needed time on her own, so she too, bought her own home. It was once again a wonderful time in my life.

Twist of Fate

Later on in that period of time, I received some *unexpected news*. A beloved and dear friend, who I had the pleasure of knowing since kindergarten, had passed away suddenly in his early forties—quite the shock, indeed. It made no sense, as I was fast approaching forty—wow, how quickly things can change!

At this point, I was thinking of making a career change. As fate would have it, an opportunity came to manage a friend's Bed and Breakfast in Byron Bay; she was going to travel overseas for a while.

Well who wouldn't want to do that? I jumped at the idea! I packed up some things and moved into my friend's adorable Bed and Breakfast, located up a quiet lane, backing onto bushland just out of the township of Byron Bay. A path meandered up the hillside of the bushland to the lighthouse. It was picturesque, and an enjoyable walk.

I was committed to my mortgage with mum. However, living in my friend's Bed and Breakfast was no outlay. I just needed to ensure her business kept the doors open, it generated an income for her, and gave her some savings whilst she travelled. I managed to do all of those things for her. It was easy. How could it not be easy? I was living in a luxurious Bed and Breakfast on the hills of Byron Bay—a life some only dream of.

Byron Bay was more authentic back in the early 90s. The major developers had not arrived as yet; it still had the ambience of a bustling hippie community; happy days!

This was another wonderful career move with a great opportunity to learn more new skills. I enjoyed several good years living here It was an exceptional lifestyle, in a stunning location, overlooking the bay. The whales and dolphins regularly swam there, and I often saw kookaburras, owls, and other beautiful birdlife enjoying the bush behind the house.

I could walk everywhere. It was an easy walk into town for supplies, and on weekends the markets flourished with fresh, healthy, locally-sourced produce. Provisioning for guests was easy and fun. The ambience was laid back. There were people singing their songs and selling the wares, a genuine community vibe.

During my time here, I was introduced to many international guests who came to stay; they had a real blast with the whales and dolphins frolicking in the bay. There were writers, artists, doctors, entrepreneurs, and many colourful people stayed with me, paving the way to experience communicating with international folk. You see, it turns out fate was setting me up for greater things to come.

During this time, the hand of fate was working its magic again. I was introduced to a friend—a local lad who grew up in Byron Bay. He was a chef and every now and then he would visit, bringing fresh local fish. At times, he would jump in and help with the cooking when needed—that is, if he wasn't working on a private yacht. He introduced me to the idea of working in the yachting industry by offering me a job as hostess.

Turns out, around the same time as my friend returned back to her Bed and Breakfast, she announced that she was putting the Bed and Breakfast on the market.

Well, guess what? I jumped at the opportunity to take up the offer to join the yacht as hostess. Who wouldn't, right? I thought this was divine timing. Fate, as you would have it, was working its magic in my life and yachting became my new career path.

I Did the Inevitable

During my time yachting in Australia, I thought to myself, *I could do this internationally. Wow!* I could travel, get paid, have somewhere to live, and have all my basic needs met, just like Island Life. I researched everything on how to, where to, and what I needed to do before I booked that flight.

I realised at the age of forty that there was a dream that I had not fulfilled as yet, and with the shock of my friends passing, it became clear to me life can be shortened unexpectedly. I said to myself, *"Don't waste time, Sue,* go ahead and follow that dream of yours. That was what prompted me to follow my dream.

I have always wanted to spend time living and experiencing Italy with its rich culture and lifestyle. It seemed now was a good a time as any to follow that dream.

Another song that awakens my spirit is from an artist I enjoy listening to.

"Don't waste time; these are the best years of our life."

by Richard Clapton.

I saw him live more than a few times. I even got to meet him, on the footpath of an Annie's Bookstore in Peregian Beach Queensland. He just released his book about his life—interesting story, worth a read.

Chapter Four
My Career in
Luxury Super Yachts

Starting out

WORKING AND LIVING ON super yachts made sense. This was how I could make this dream of mine possible. I didn't travel to Italy right away, but *in time, I did.*

Yes, I did the inevitable. I booked a flight to Florida, organised a crew house to stay in, and made an appointment with a yacht agency to find work—all with bare minimal money in my bank account. Bearing in mind, I was still committed to a mortgage with my mum. However, the excitement of this new adventure overruled reason. I had a dream to fulfil.

I put myself out on a limb so I could experience life in new locations—kind of like a spiritual pilgrimage. I worked through daily life experiences to learn more about who I was in essence. I know it sounds cliché, yet it is actually how I have lived my life.

It was time to travel a long way from home; far from the comfort of family and the convenience of being in Australia. All my emotions were moving around in me; so much so, I swear if my skin wasn't holding them in, they would be all over the place, *seriously*. I have now landed on international soil, and it was quite surreal. "Hello" to the USA and the beginning of a new chapter in my life—*oh my goodness*. Sue, this is not really a good time to be saying, *"What was I thinking?"*

Arriving in Fort Lauderdale, Florida in the midst of summer was overwhelming to say the least. Who said it was a good time to travel here in the summer? It's as hot as far North Queensland, yikes!

Since I was looking to start a career in the luxurious world of super yachts, summer was the best time to find a suitable yacht to join and start my new career path.

In reality, I was in a foreign land looking for work in an environment in which I had a bare minimal knowledge. A hint of fear popped up. At this phase of the journey, I didn't know a soul here or anywhere remotely close by. *Oh, so quickly this reality sets in!*

Feeling totally alone, somewhat dazed and tired from a long flight, with the light of the sun shining on my face so brightly, the heat beating upon my body, I perspired profusely; to the point my clothes stuck to my skin. I knew that the feeling of anxiety was adding to this experience, as I felt completely overwhelmed.

On that day, I used all forms of transport—planes, trains, and automobiles.

From the baggage claim area, I pull out my notes with directions to the crew accommodation I found online. My heart pounded with a feeling of anxiousness.

I dragged my suitcases out of the airport terminal onto a shuttle bus that would take me across the entire terminal to the train station—way over the other side. On the train, the air conditioning brought a slight reprieve. I settled into a chair, looked through the dusty windows at this new terrain, and pondered my thoughts in the beginning of this new adventure. On my way to the crew house, I thought this would be a good base while I looked for a suitable yacht to join. At least a crew house would have like-minded people with whom I could share the beginning of this adventure. Well that's what I thought!

Eventually, I arrived at Fort Lauderdale station to be greeted by the lady who manages this crew house—quite a character she is; not the least bit friendly or helpful. She greeted me with a limited smile with no warmth or hospitality anywhere to be seen. Instead, she watched me struggle to lift my suitcases into the boot of the car. She was more interested in correcting me, pointing out that in America, it's called a trunk, not a boot.

Feeling somewhat surprised at my initial contact, I couldn't help but see the humour, as the more I asked her for information about where I could buy the basics of food, water, and wine nearby, she showed very little interest in sharing this information. She preferred telling me about the rules she had laid down and not to lose the key as she would not take a call if I locked myself out.

An interesting start to say the least, but it doesn't stop there, oh no. We arrived at a rambling older style house. The garden had much to be desired, and the rickety path to the front door was quite a safety hazard, especially with limited light to show you where to step in the dark. She opened the door, stepped in before me to look around, and conducted a brief chat of the rules again. Then, she rushed out the door and it slammed shut. I guessed she was gone then. What a funny lady; I had to laugh.

Drop the suitcases, put on walking shoes, don't forget the key; *I chuckled to myself* as I walked outside with the idea there has to be a shop nearby for supplies. Turned out the shop was a long way from the house. I started walking more than an hour ago and it was dark, but I felt pleased to be back safely.

At this stage, I had no access to a phone, which made me somewhat nervous. Once I was back, I poured myself that much-needed glass of vino, and I sat down, looking around my new surrounds, only to realise it is very quiet for a large home of eight bedrooms. Wow, there is no one else here and I was completely alone. This was not my intention. The idea of staying in a crew house was to meet people.

To clarify, at this stage my experience with technology was limited. My basic understanding of needing a mobile phone was one thing, but I had no idea it needed to be unlocked. Even so, coming to Florida with an unlocked phone was ok, but I had to sign up with a provider, just to be able to use the phone. I knew this would not work well, as living on board a yacht meant I have no fixed address and we would be in and out of countries that all required their own sim cards. This was a learning curve for me, especially as technology was still fairly new for the everyday person.

At this, stage to make a call, I had to buy calling cards to make a call. It seems antiquated; however this is how it was. Skyping from your phone and seeing the person you were talking to was not yet an option, but it did come in time.

International banking, too, had not yet become available. In order to transfer money home to Australia—for the mortgage I am committed to—I needed to open a bank account in the USA, then I had to come into the bank and ask for help to wire money, to obtain all these numbers, and sign all this paperwork. It was a process, indeed!

It was even more challenging to open a bank account, as I was obviously not from Florida, nor did I have a full time job. These few technical issues challenged me in those early days. I needed money to go home to Australia regularly, and going into a bank to wire money was not always possible when you were never in one place or even nearby a place—let alone the same bank, as you are most likely on anchor or tied to a dock in another country, anyway.

Everything happens for a reason

Upon my return, by chance, there was a guy there, who just arrived from Canada and he too, was seeking a career in super yachts. *Thank you!* My first sign! He became a valuable friend. During those early days of yachting, we shared many a yachting experience. It appeared as though the hand of fate was setting this new adventure.

My journey unfolded quickly, as I landed my first job on a large yacht. Wow, this is great! I met a couple, by chance, via my new Canadian friend; they also were new to the industry, and seeking work. I was able to assist them, *and as it turned out,* they assisted me. I found them day work on the yacht—thank goodness, because when I was fired *for stating I did not trust the chief stewardess' intentions,* I needed somewhere to live. They were now my new flatmates. This chance connection has given me clarity that things were happening for a reason.

Shortly after, my new flatmates found work on-board a yacht and it was time for me now to find another crew house. By chance, at the next crew house I moved into, I met a captain, who happened to be on days off. He became the most integral part of this journey; actually, he is my best friend to this day. By chance, Captain Al had a studio in Fort Lauderdale and a car—thank you, Universe!—as this became a saving grace, a home away from home, when I was in between yachts.

I quickly learnt that in between yachts is typical of the industry. He introduced to me to this amazing woman, who lives in Fort Lauderdale with her husband and two dogs. Her heart opened wide to me, and she invited me into her home when I needed a friend. We enjoyed lengthy conversations of life experiences, beauty treatments, leisurely lunches, and champagne. This amazing woman has become a valuable friend. I know her to be my family overseas; Bell is my best friend today.

Meanwhile, I found a new yacht to join, and *of course Captain Al was available, to* take me to Miami airport to meet my second yacht, based in St Lucia. I was flown to St Lucia. Another part of this career I learned about, is the fact that you are flown to meet the yacht, leave the yacht, and for interviews—wow, an interesting lifestyle!

What a majestic sight upon arrival into the airport of St Lucia. It is a beautiful island in the southern part of the Caribbean Islands, which has, to this day, an active volcano. The volcano

St Lucia The Pitons

stands up above the ocean in all its glory, just like the first time I saw Lord Howe Island. A *surreal* moment that made my heart flutter, as this sight of St Lucia, was similar to the visual I saw on my first voyage. That first visual of Lord Howe Island is what inspired me to travel abroad and join the world of luxury yachting, and here I am, living that dream.

Early days in St Lucia, I met a Spanish man who lives there; he became a valuable new friend. We got on well; he knew many the locals, as he has lived here in Marigot Bay for quite some time. He was very social and introduced me to some wonderful and colourful folk. He is an amazing artist. We enjoyed many adventures around the island.

Apparently, I was too social in the community of St Lucia for the captain of this yacht, and as it turned out, I was fired. Yes, I was fired from my first two yachts—bit of an awkward start, indeed. It seemed I had a bit to learn about this new yachting world. As I was driven to make this idea work, each

Marigot Bay St Lucia water taxi

experience that was unfolding—good and not—did not stop me. Doors were opening, along this new pathway and some incredible strangers became the most valuable friends.

From my experience, nothing is by chance; everything happens to connect you to a more meaningful part of yourself.

The chief stewardess from the first yacht who had me fired because I didn't trust her intentions, also managed to have that Captain, first mate, and engineer fired. Listening to my instincts has served me well. Sometimes, speaking out your thoughts does not turn out for the better right away. Later, I heard that the second captain who fired me was fired too, and when we met up again, he was apologetic for that experience.

Would this not be serendipitous to meet up again and hear these stories?

Experience becomes knowledge; knowledge once integrated becomes wisdom.

Valuable Friends

This valuable new Spanish friend Juan supported me and suggested I stay with him until I built my confidence, before I fly back to the USA. So I went to the airport to change my flight, which was difficult. In this case, the flights were booked via a booking agent and couldn't be changed. Sheer determination on my behalf, I changed my flight for a week later. I phoned Juan, to say I was on my way back to his home in Marigot Bay, shaking from the shock of all this unravelling before me.

Wow, not only had I been fired twice, for the first time in my career; I was now driving back to stay with a man I barely knew, nearby the yacht I had just been fired from, whilst riding in a taxi with a man who drove like he was crazed. We went so fast up and down those narrow roads that I prayed I would arrive safely. When I arrived, Juan was madly rushing around with a mop, cleaning his home.

"I don't normally do this, however, I wanted to make my home comfortable for you," he said as he greeted me. When he welcomed me into his home, with his adorable Spanish accent, he spoke with the words of an archangel. "Bella, you stay here until you have strength in your confidence, to start again."

He, too, opened his home to me. I was discovering that this was how things happened, when you trusted in others you met by chance. He too is my friend to this day.

Upon my return to the USA, I contacted Captain Al. *Of course*, he was in Florida, and available to pick me up from the airport. He confirmed his home was available, and I could stay as long as I needed, anytime. He invited me to join him for a much needed beer and he shared his stories of yachting—just the inspiration I needed to continue.

Lifestyle On-board

What an exceptional lifestyle, living in a world of ultimate luxury with the best of everything at your fingertips—Lear jets, private helicopters flying in and landing on the deck of the yacht, blacked out stretch limousines, traveling to exotic locations, earning fabulous money and mind-blowing tips—fun was easily created. Life was filled with adventure after adventure. I thought I had found the ultimate vocation.

It started off with a bit of a hiccup; however. I very quickly learnt there are certain ethics of working and living in this luxurious environment for the rich and famous. A good majority of it is about the image—and that included the captain and crew, not just the owners and their guests. Privacy and discretion was paramount at all times—on and off the yacht.

Crewing in the luxurious world of super yachts, traveling the world, living within the realm of wealth that is unimaginable to most, opened my eyes. I am blessed with a career in luxury yachting that has carried me over ten years. Even today as I share my story with you in this book, I am still living in a world filled with decadence, excess, glitz, glam, and lots of razzle dazzle.

Mind you, it certainly does have its fair share of tales full of adventure, romance, and chance meetings, blended with a colourful array of people. At times, confined to the small spaces of the crew area, gives plenty of room for the unexpected. Many, many wonderful and transforming experiences are illuminated in the oddest of places. Living within the luxurious world of the rich and famous is not all it appears to be.

There are many more tales of adventure in the nitty gritty of living and working on-board, jam packed together, within the unique environment and lifestyle of super yachts. I could write a whole book on this alone. It would be fun to reconnect with some of the people I met and worked with during my ten-year career of luxury international yachting. Who knows, they may wish to add some stories of their experiences into my book.

Chapter Five
My Travel Destinations

NOW WE ARE HERE, let's talk about the travel.

My First Voyage

I will always remember my first voyage from Brisbane to Lord Howe Island. As the sun shed light where, a few hours ago, there was nothing but stars and the ocean floor. A sight I had never experienced before stood before me as we approached Lord Howe Island. It was the first time my eyes had seen anything as magical or as majestic as that piece of land. It just stood there, jutting out of the ocean floor. With that vision, my inspiration zoomed forward to travel with super yachts internationally. I wanted more.

Around the Globe

Since that day, I have been to some beautiful places around the globe. Upon flying into Fort Lauderdale, a whole world of travel opened up for me. I had the opportunity to visit places I never imagined possible. There is Miami just south of Fort Lauderdale, and Sarasota on the South West Coast of Florida. South of Fort Lauderdale is Key Largo and Key West—party town haven, with so many great bars, live music everywhere, the extensive beverage menus with cocktails galore, and each place offering specials to entice the visitors. The food is yummy—especially the Key Lime Pie and the diving is amazing.

From Key West, USA, it is an easy trip to the Bahamas. Bimini was our first port we stopped to enjoy for a week and then we journeyed downward to Atlantis Resort at Nassau. This is the main island in the Bahamas and a very popular hub for super yachts. That is only part of the Bahamas. When you leave the glitz and glam of Atlantis and travel south to the islands, a whole new world opens up. It is like a forgotten era in time, raw in its natural beauty, crystal clear waters, and to this day, mostly untouched. Celebrities have private islands with luxury homes on these islands. Lucky them, I say, as it is one of my most favourite places in the world, and the epitome of yachting.

Atlantis Resort Nassua Bahamas

MY TRAVEL DESTINATIONS

Nassua Bahamas Beach Bar

Island in the Bahamas

Mariner in the Bahamas

Jamaica local shop

On one particular trip, the seas were becoming rough—my term for it is "getting *pretty crazy out here*". The seafaring captain and engineer saw it differently. We were on our way to Aruba, part of the ABC islands in the southern part of the Caribbean. North of Venezuela, the island of Aruba is famous for its stunning blonde beaches and wind-sculpted desert landscapes. Cacti are part of the landscape with some of the best wreck diving in the Caribbean. Aruba is a relatively dry island with consistently fine weather. We enjoyed some beach buggy action on the beach. There are some amazing caves to check out.

As the seas had taken a turn for the worst, we needed to find a place of cover. The engineer suggested Jamaica; *of course you do, this is yachting*. Turns out, six weeks later, we are still tied to a dock in Jamaica. Happy days!

Who would have thought I'd be hanging out in Jamaica? Once the sea had settled—*or should I say in my terms, I was told it had*—onward to Aruba we went. I guess everyone's idea of settled down is vastly different to mine... Got to love your first experience of seasick—*not good*.

I've been to Los Roques; it is a remote set of islands, above South America, with a glorious reef system and some spectacular diving. We hung out here, as it is close enough for the boss to fly in and out of, on his private helicopter. Hanging out in exotic locations long enough, you will find out all sorts of things. The world is full of amazing locations and by yacht, it opens up another dimension. I loved it here, for a place made up of islands and coral reef, it is a lovely surprise to see it thriving on every level, and this is a highlight for me.

The Los Roques islands are a federal dependency of Venezuela, consisting of about 350 islands, cays, or islets. The most important island is Gran Roque, as it's the only populated island in the group and has an airport suitable for small

Gran Roque village

Gran Roque Alas Mosquitos

aircraft. Other important islands for visitors are Francisqui, Nordisqui, Madrisqui, and Crasqui.

The archipelago itself is located about eighty miles (128 km) directly north of the port of La Guairá, and from there it's a forty-minute flight to Gran Roque.

Basically an untouched coral reef, it attracts many visitors, especially from Europe, some of which come in their own yachts and anchor in the inner, protected, shallow waters. However, development and tourism are aggressively controlled by the government. Because of the wide variety of seabirds and rich aquatic life, the Venezuelan government declared Los Roques a National Park in 1972.

Onward bound to St Maarten another *very popular* place for super yachts, mega yachts, and the crew, too. If you haven't seen friends you have met during your yachting career in a while, chances are you will see them here; most likely in a Caribbean-style bar, dotted on a beach somewhere on St Maarten. Arriving into St Maarten is a spectacular sight, with all these huge yachts on anchor in Simpson Bay; *they simply won't fit in the mariner, yeah right!*

It is true they are huge. St Maarten is a fun place to hang out, with its collective mix of bars; the most popular ones brim with character. These bars are built mostly from colourful and rustic timber, and positioned right on the beach. If you want a little dancing in the night, there are some funky lounge bars, nightclubs and a casino—always plenty to do when you don't have guests on-board.

Nearby, there is St Barts, which is known for being a bit of a challenge to tie up to—to say the least—and the yachts are crammed in tight. Not far from St Barts are Tortola and the British Virgin Islands, another really pretty destination.

Did I really do all that traveling?
As it turns out, I have; but wait, there's more.

Isla Mujeres Mexico

Isla Mujeres Mexico

La Paz Marina Mexico

There are more wonderful travel destinations

Over to Mexico, and the stunning island called Isla Mujeres—the name means Island of women—in the Caribbean Sea. I enjoyed a few spectacular dives here.

(http://www.isla-mujeres.net/)

On the other side of Mexico is La Paz, north of Cabo St Lucas, on in the Baja California Peninsula, another popular tourist destination. Both locations are stunning, yet vastly different in their landscaping and lifestyle.

(http://www.allaboutcabo.com/)

The captain and first mate on one of the yachts I lived on had friends who crewed on sports fishing yachts. They were hanging out on the mainland of Mexico just south of Cancun. There are huge resorts dotted along the coastline each of which opens up to a world all of its own.

La Paz Mexico

We had a few days off, so the Captain decided it would be fun to enjoy a road trip south to meet up with their friends. As we were based in Isla Mujeres, it was just a quick boat trip over to the mainland, to hire a car, pick up supplies, and then head south. From here, the world opens up. The drive is beautiful, *and of course*, another adventure unfolded.

We arrived to the mariner through the Palatial Resort, in Puerto Aventuras Mexico, to where their buddies were based for the fishing season. As we came around to the mariner, from where we parked the car, I could see for miles, a stunning array of *fancy* looking Sport Fishing yachts, all backed onto the dock. Wow, this is another realm to yachting I had not seen!

It was certainly not like the super yachts I had been crewing on. The crew here were very laid back, obviously settled into the Mexican lifestyle. It is a social hub, and everyone enjoyed a good time. The crew have set up music, barbecues and tables, all covered over with marquis—not just to keep the food and beverages cold, but also to bring everyone together.

These folk were polite, courteous, and incredibly laid back. What a pleasant change from the "upkeep" lifestyle of super yachts.

I love Mexico; the culture, the locals, the way of life, the margaritas—it has a laid back kind of vibe to it. The gypsy in me is at home in this environment. The captain suggested I have a look around while they head out for a fish. "OK, Captain! As you say!" *Captain's orders it is*, I chuckled to myself as I headed off to explore.

I thought to myself I had better do what the locals do; find a shady place, sit down, and order a cold beverage. The first bar I found was full of character, just like you see in the movies—a rustic timber shack, palm trees, and sand surrounded the coloured bar, giving you that laid-back kind of feel. This reminded me of a song I love by Kenny Chesney, as I can relate

Puerto Aventuras Mexico

to the lyrics as I ponder my life at times. It is called "Beer in Mexico". It was playing as I approached the red timber shack called Gringos Bar, and I felt drawn to sit down and listen.

As I sat myself down on a timber stool at the bar, the barman, a friendly chap—quite the character – greeted me. He asked where I was from, as he introduced himself to me. He said he was from America and his name was Tarzan—*of course it was! I had a chuckle, because what else could you say to that*?

He was a solid hunk of a guy, so the name was quite fitting; however, it did make for some fun banter across the bar for a few hours. Turns out the captain was out fishing longer than I had anticipated. However, they were gone long enough for me to meet quite a few of the local folk, and everyone loved my Aussie accent and we all enjoyed a few rounds of margaritas.

When the Captain returned from fishing, he thought he had better come look for me. As he turned the corner, he could see I had made myself quite at home, sitting among the locals, laughing, and sharing stories, as I sipped on margaritas. He chuckled to himself as he approached.

"I will never need to worry about you, Sue. You make friends easily." He sat down, and before he opened his mouth, a cold beer was in front of him. That's how it is down here in Mexico.

I have fond memories of Mexico, especially with this captain and first mate; they were salt of the earth, good, kind-hearted people. I felt blessed to have shared time on-board with this team. More tales of adventures were born here, that is for certain.

I was still with the same captain and first mate team when we left Mexico to head over to the Cayman Islands. I had an opportunity to swim with the stingrays—an interesting experience to say the least. There are 365 dive spots in the Cayman Islands; you could dive in a different place every day of the year.

Cayman Islands swimming with the sting rays

http://caymanislands.com/

We crossed a part of the Bermuda Triangle at night. On watch, you have to listen out for anything unusual. During my four-hour watch—which was 12am to 4am—with the captain, we heard some interesting conversations on the radio.

One conversation we listened to, indicated there was a "mayday" of a sailing yacht that had capsized. It was a long way from where we were, so the conversation was not clear. There was another announcement. A yacht was lost, the weather was deteriorating fast, and the GPS was not working.

That night the sky was misty and the fog was rolling in. You could barely see the stars. It was eerie, and we were grateful we were safely underway.

We arrived in the afternoon to Bermuda and dropped anchor in a picturesque bay on the southern end. The Captain says, "Just enough light for a water ski—who is up for it?" The crew all jumped at the idea. Playtime is part of what makes this career so interesting. The beaches here are stunning, one of the differences here is some of the beaches give a pink look, which is caused by tiny red organisms that grow beneath the coral reefs just off the shore. When they die and fall to the ocean floor, the organisms mingle with bits of coral and crushed shell that are washed onto the beach and make the sand appear an otherworldly shade of pink. Not all of Bermuda's beaches are pink.

I was flown in to join a yacht based in Newport, Rhode Island. This was a very memorable and wonderful experience. The yacht was ultra-modern, a bit like a big fancy speedboat with a Jacuzzi on the top deck. It was brand new with fresh, modern, and comfortable decor. To my surprise, it had a huge crew mess, with modern cabins and a porthole to see to the outside world. As the yacht was based in Newport, Rhode Island, the cruising locations for the owners and their guests were Martha's Vineyard and Nantucket; both located south of Cape Cod in Massachusetts, it is likened to an bygone era.

The chief stewardess greeted me on arrival. I was pleased to meet a lady full of life, who was happy and enjoyed being social. What a blessing to have met a real down-to-earth lady from North Carolina. We shared similar interests, such as going to the theatre, watching movies, listening to music, all the arts, good healthy food and delicious beverages, and shopping.

Newport, Rhode Island http://cityofnewport.com/ is a historic township with its talk of ghost stories. My highlight was the old castles, which were really mansions, with their exquisitely landscaped gardens along the ocean shore line.

We would walk along the shore line most days. You could walk for miles. It was stunning to see history still loud and clear along these rocky edges; it is beautiful indeed. The town is filled with character; there are quirky bars, live music, and a choice of garden bars sprawling down to the waterfront, playing live music. It has a really old movie theatre and of course fabulous shopping. I fell in love with the area; I will go back there one day.

This, for me, was a feel-good experience; I was on the yacht with a great crew, and off the yacht with a land-based lifestyle, there are many fabulous walks, and ample places to explore. There is so much you can do in this region. As the yacht was based here, it gave the crew more of a land-based lifestyle.

The chief stewardess had friends who lived nearby. I was introduced on many an social occasion, which opened doors for friendships to be made, adventures to be had, and good times to be experienced all round.

New York was only a train trip away. We enjoyed several weekends in New York. I loved the city's buzzing atmosphere, which was alive anytime of the day and into the night.

A friend was on his way back to Newport, RI and offered to pick us up from New York on his way through. While we were waiting, we discovered a fabulous funky bar, just below the building we stayed in. What a good find! It was pumping with people and live music mid-morning. When he arrived, he chuckled, and said, "You girls, you certainly know how to have fun. I am here to pick you up, ladies. Are you ready for an adventure? I am taking you on road trip; there will be a few detours on the way back to Newport RI."

Yes, of course we were! What fun—another adventure? I enjoyed these new friends; we had some wonderful, fun filled adventures.

> *As I bring back all these wonderful memories into the pages of this book, I am in awe of all the amazing locations I have visited, the friends I made, and the life I led.*

Traveling Around Australia

I've also had the opportunity to travel the East Coast of Australia on yachts.

The memory of the morning we arrived at Lord Howe Island will always be clear in my mind. How spectacular it looked! Only with yachting can you experience such a scene upon arrival, especially after days and days at sea, looking at only the vastness of the ocean floor and stars in the night sky. This, for me, was the moment that inspired me to find a career in luxury super yachting and travel the globe.

During the early days of yachting in Australia, based on the Gold Coast and Brisbane, was an incredible start, especially getting my sea legs and a great learning platform before I set off into the big wide world of yachting internationally. It was very different to Australian standards.

To begin, I enjoyed cruising the Broadwater, Tangalooma, Moreton Bay, and Stradbroke Island—each with its own beauty. Then onward bound to Sydney Harbour.

We arrived late in the evening on a full moon. Wow! Stunning entrance into the harbour indeed! Then, finally, we have a calm day to travel up to Pittwater. On the way up, I saw a Hammerhead shark cruising alongside the yacht.

It did not stop there. There was plenty more to come, as we headed south to Mornington Peninsula, Adelaide, and all the way down to Kangaroo Island.

It is here I had the opportunity to experience the lifestyle of the rich. The owner had an eight-seater helicopter which flies in and lands on the middle deck of the yacht, as we cruise slowly at minimal speed, and apparently, it makes it easier to land. The yacht is well fitted out to accommodate this helicopter. What a spectacular sight watching this happen in front of me. The pilot disembarks and joins the guests on-board for the night. Meanwhile, the helicopter sits there in all its glory until the boss chooses to take it for a cruise—*as you do,* living in the world of super yachts.

Whitsunday Islands Great Barrier Reef

Hayman Island Whitsunday Islands

Lucky me! Guess who received the enviable invitation to go for a cruise in the eight-seater helicopter? Yes, that'd be me, with all the crew. We flew over Kangaroo Island for a good hour—spectacular! I was in awe, as we took off from the deck of the

Gove Northern Territory

Gove Northern Territory

yacht, and then watched as we landed back on the yacht. It was an amazing experience to say the least.

Next, we headed north to Airlie Beach, Cairns, Hamilton Island, Hayman Island, and Whitehaven beach in the Whitsundays. I learnt to dive in the Great Barrier Reef, *as you do. It appears a bit of the luxury rubbed off on me.*

Most of the Australian yachts end up at Lizard Island; it is remote here, like your own private oasis. During another trip, we headed further north, to the top of Australia, for Barramundi fishing in Gove, Northern Territory.

How could I forget Fiji?

Never! It is stunning—the water, diving, scenery. Another Australian yacht I crewed on was based down in the island of Fiji, where the owner bought an island and built a resort.

As you do, in the elite world of the luxury

Fiji - Bar in middle of Ocean

Chapter Six
Dreams Really Do Come True

THANKS TO MY CAREER in luxury yachting, I enjoyed plenty of European travel, but most importantly, I had the opportunity to embrace my dream to visit Italy.

Landing in Florence, Italy

Finally, I lived to experience my dream: to visit Italy and experience its culture and lifestyle.

To quote—This is how I enjoyed the adventure I called "Travel To Live". For me it is the true meaning of how I live my life and how the name of my book came about.

I chose to do this as a personal journey, not on yacht. As I flew into Florence, Italy, my heart was pounding, my palms sweaty, and the excitement was oozing out of me. I felt like a kid in a lolly shop for the first time.

Il Duomo Florence Italy

I had booked an apartment online and wasn't quite sure what to expect. It was late when I arrived and already dark, so I couldn't really see exactly where I was. To my surprise, when I woke up to the morning light through the dusty window, I could see Il Duomo in the city of Florence, with the sun glistening upon it. This was my vision; this is what I saw in my mind's eye, of my dream to travel to Italy.

Wow, I was really here. My skin was tingling with goose bumps all over. It was a dream come true.

Exploring Florence through to Ventimiglia, Italy

I spent three months travelling through Italy and the surrounding regions. I always dreamed of visiting Italy.

Tuscany was one place on my list to visit. As I was based in Florence, I thought that hiring a car from would be the best way to see as much as I could. I didn't really get lost; I just couldn't read Italian. The names could have said anything. I didn't really mind, as I was living my dream. I took off toward any signs I could read that lead to Tuscany.

High up into the snow-capped mountains I went, into the quaintest of villages, with bubbling brooks along the roadside. It was incredible to be on this adventure. I saw some amazing countryside.

The excitement at times overwhelmed me. I simply wanted to stop everywhere, have a walk around, and of course, try the local vino. I stayed in authentic accommodation in the villages I drove through.

At times, speaking the language was awkward, to say the least. This became obvious the further inland from the coast I drove. The way of life in the villages is more authentic, and less tainted by the tourism industry. I found that most Italians welcomed my hand gestures, my warm smile, and an attempt

Tuscany region Italy

Cinque Terre Monterosso

at speaking Italian. Eventually, my communication was understood.

Days later, I popped out at Viareggio, a beautiful seaside township, and a hub where large yachts had maintenance work done. It is here I said goodbye to the car and jumped on the train so I could take in more of the scenery. From Viareggio, I headed north toward La Spezia, then onto Cinque Terre, five villages on the hillside of the Italian Riviera coastline.

Arriving at Cinque Terre is a sight to behold. The view from the train window is incredible, and each village is unique. I felt an urge to head across to Monterosso to look for accommodation. I based myself here for six weeks. What appealed to me is the variety of walking trails connecting all the villages. It is a world heritage site and it is incredibly beautiful. The people are friendly and there is so much to explore.

I loved the fact, it was easy to navigate and the train station is there, if I didn't want to walk. The town was bustling; there were markets in the Piazza, some really funky bars to hang out in, delicious food everywhere, and I felt safe here.

How my accommodation came about was remarkable, and I felt truly blessed. I was walking around Monterosso with my suitcase in tow, thinking of accommodation. Where, what type, how can I make this happen and at a price I could afford? As this was a high visitation region, the prices are high, too.

I walked into a quaint but gorgeous boutique hotel, full of character. Nearby was the most beautiful beach, and it was within walking distance to everything I could ever need. It was perfect.

"Well, go on, Sue," I said to myself. "You are here now, just ask."

The lady who greeted me was the owner of the hotel; she was friendly with clear spoken English. I asked her of accommodation and explained that I wanted to stay for a few months, and need a place that was self-contained. Turns out, her mother used to live in the apartment below the hotel, which had a door from the laneway.

"I will take you there," she said. She stopped what she is doing, we walked outside the hotel, downs the steps onto the street, and then we turned to walk up the lane to a big timber door that sat right on the laneway. She opened the door, and to my amazement, a gorgeous home was presented to me. She said her mother has not lived here for some time, so it was a bit dusty. She promised to have the cleaners of the hotel take care of it, if I wanted the apartment.

If I like it? I said, "Yes, of course! It is adorable!" Oh, wait a minute . . . I have not asked how much it is. I felt no need for concern, my gut feelings were bubbling inside me, and the hand of fate was working with me on that day. Turns out, magic

Monterosso, Italy. My Accommodation for 6 weeks.

was at hand. It was at a price I could afford, it is fully self-contained, including linen, and I could move in today. Wow, how blessed I felt this day! I enjoyed a memorable six weeks living in Monterosso, one of the five villages in the Cinque Terre, Italian Riviera, on the Amalfi coast. Cinque Terre has now become one of my favourite destinations in Italy.

Monterosso is picturesque; I loved it. There is so much to enjoy here, and the township is filled with character and old-world charm. The cobbled laneways in and around the town are like a time gone by. I felt inspired by the history in the buildings and pathways that lead up to the top of the cliffs, the views on the way to the top are breathtaking. No wonder I stayed for six weeks; it felt like I was at home here. At one of the quaint bars, I met some other wandering travellers who were staying in the next town for a few days. We spent some time together eating and drinking and sharing stories of our adventures as we ventured around the region.

Monterosso Train Station Cinque Terre

It was time to move on. I have booked accommodation in Ventimiglia, on the border of Italy and France. At the train station in Monterosso, I discovered a delicious vino; a sparkling rosé with a screw top lid, but not as bubbly. I bought a glass and sat on the terrace of the station, pondering my adventure so far, as I overlooked the ocean.

The train station was picturesque. There were pots filled with colourful flowers and hanging pot plants. That is what I love about Italy; there are coloured flowers and plants hanging everywhere. The location inspires me very much. I love the train travel in Italy, because it is easy.

Ventimiglia is a city in Liguria, northern Italy, in the Province of Imperia. I arrived at the train station, only to realise my accommodation is way up on the top of the hill. Ventimiglia is mostly Italian speaking, with very little English—as for me, I am the complete opposite. Oh, well, got this far—I was sure I could organise a taxi, once I worked out what that was called.

The road to the place where I was staying was really steep, narrow, and windy. I felt a bit dizzy by the time we approached the top. I would not be planning a leisurely walk down the road anytime soon; I just hoped there was a bus.

The lady who greeted me spoke very little English, and with my limited Italian, it made for an awkward exchange. In this case, I needed to arrange for someone to meet me and give me a key to the cottage. As I have booked it online, I thought I had taken care of that part. There was a bit of confusion, as she was not expecting my arrival. Fortunately for me, she was home. As we tried to communicate, we saw there was some uncertainty about the duration and the dates that I planned to be stay. Oh, my! But in the end, we stayed there. That's a good thing, as I have booked to stay two weeks.

Ventimiglia is an old town, it is on the edge of Italy, and the first town visitors see when they enter the country from France. It has a character unlike any other Riviera town, retaining its traditional identity while adopting an eclectic selection of the new. There's none of the glitz and glamour of its neighbours, instead it's an honest, understated yet comfortable place to visit, explore or just be. (http://ventimiglia.town/)

There was no glitz and glam; it was an authentic part of Italy, somewhat rustic. This was what I enjoyed about the city of Ventimiglia. The food was really good, in keeping with traditional style. There was pizza, pasta dishes, olives, antipasto, crusty bread dipped in oil, croissants filled with Nutella, strong coffee—just plain, good Italian food. Each place I went into to eat offered a glass of vino or a shot of coffee, usually with a little taste morsel to enjoy with it.

From Ventimiglia, I travelled by train to San Remo, Genoa, La Spezia, and onto Siena, Pisa. As Ventimiglia is on the border of France, this opened up another region to view. Why not enjoy it while I was there?

Across the Border into France and Spain

Across the border I went to France, passing along Mento and Monaco, through Nice toward Antibes. Antibes is a very large super and mega yacht haven—one of the largest in the world.

The day I walked into the harbour was a sight indeed. I thought this visual was only in movies. I have never seen so many yachts, let alone, imagine the size of them. And not just a few; there were hundreds of these huge yachts. Wow, I felt like I had been living under a rock; this was serious wealth.

I wandered around the edge of the mariner, not game to step inside to where the yachts were. It was still a bit daunting, so I left the mariner and headed into the town of Antibes. What a gorgeous town; it also had a charming blend of old-world charm and modern convenience. The narrow streets, cobbled laneways, and flower pots hanging from the terraces—it is pretty.

Antibes May 09

This day, the market place was alive with people. There was an abundance of fresh produce, an incredible display of colourful spices, bottles filled with all sorts of delicious treasures—you could easily provision here for your guests. A fun and very social town, there were yacht crews everywhere, enjoying the convenience of the proximity to the mariner. Hanging out in one of these bars, I was sure I would eventually run into someone I know.

I took a trip up to Biot, a pretty village only one train station away from Antibes. I short bus trip up the hill behind Biot, there is an exquisite historic village in the hills – it had so much character, and once again the food was yummy. As I was mixing around the yachting hubs—that's where the crews hang out—you are bound to run into friends. I met up with some friends, and we enjoyed a lovely lunch at an authentic Crepe café. It was so good that I enjoyed a starter, main, and a desert, all washed down deliciously with a lovely French rosé—it was a taste sensation!

Staying in Ventimiglia, with this at your door, made it easy to explore the area. Over the weeks, I went to Cannes, Toulon, Marseille, and Montpellier.

It was time to move again; this time I am was an adventure to Palma de Mallorca. It was easy to train it everywhere. I boarded a train in Ventimiglia and headed south to Barcelona, Spain, followed by an overnight ferry to Palma de Mallorca. I spent a few weeks in Palma de Mallorca. From there, I hired a car and had a good look around. Here, the mariners are also filled with fancy super and mega yachts. This is an amazing world of luxury; there is no shortage of wealth in this world. Some of the yachts have helicopters sitting on the top, shining in all their glory, as they wait to fly off to some exotic location.

Visiting Italy was the highlight of my life. It is my dream, which has manifested today. It is here where I enjoyed the most amazing and wonderful journey. This was not just a pre-planned holiday; it was an adventure, and a dream comes true. This is what I wanted to do and here I am *living my dream*. In order for me to fully embrace this realisation, I wanted to let the gypsy in me live freely in her dream. To let the carefree spirit in my heart enjoy the adventure; to experience the culture and the lifestyle. Who knew it would have led to this?

I am still in awe. Dreams really do come true.

When you want something enough, you have to believe. Do not lose sight. Maintain your focus. Let go of the 'how?', and trust in the inevitable. Follow your heart's guidance

Chapter Seven

References

THANK YOU FOR PICKING up this book and reading it through up to here.

I do have a question for you.

If you were the reference reading your own book, what would you say to yourself? If you knew being you was enough and that your story does matter; if you could help even just one person, would you do it?

Are you brave enough to be the storyteller of your life and let the world know who you are?

Would you take the risk of looking like a fool, acting reckless in the desire to follow your dream and live the adventure of being alive?

I believe everyone has a story of value and meaning. If you could be brave enough to share it, you may be surprised how many people you could help on their journey.

The Proof is in this Book

The power of the written word can help us all. This has been proven time and time again.

I wrote this book as a reminder of the commitment I have made to myself, to live the life I dreamed of and let the Gypsy in me live freely in many directions. It is upon writing this book of my search for the ultimate vocation. It now makes sense what that means to me.

Now, you may be wondering where I found the time to write. I actually broke my shoulder, pretty badly, and needed a complete shoulder reconstruction. I had to commit to a full-on rehabilitation for the healing process and could not return to my current job as Chief Stewardess in Luxury Yachting. During rehabilitation, I realised the extent of my injury and it appeared I had to change career paths and try to find something else to do. Meanwhile as part of the rehab I needed to go back to work, but as I could not go back to yachting, I decided to volunteer with a company that helps those with disabilities and mental health issues get back into the work force and back into community.

I am not one for sitting around feeling sorry for myself. I thought well I have always wanted to write a book about my career path and what brought me to this day. As I saw it, now was a good time to do this. Because I could not use my arm, as it was damaged badly, Google Drive was my best friend, I could speak into the doc and it would put it in text format. My message to you is, you can do anything you dream of, regardless of where you are at! If I let my injury hold me back and if I did not believe in my abilities to write a book, I would most likely still be thinking about doing it, in place I have fulfilled that dream!

This is my vocation, I am the storyteller of my own life, this is who I am, it is here in these pages I share that dream with you.

Who would have thought it was possible—from sitting in my home on the Gold Coast, Australia, wondering how was I was going to bring my dream into reality, to experience Italy, learn its culture, and enjoy the adventure? Now here I am, living proof.

I feel blessed to have had this experience; it has opened my eyes *widely*, touched my heart *dearly,* and enlightened my soul. As it turns out, I have fulfilled more than one dream: to visit Italy *and* to write this book. I realise that pursuing one created the other.

Acknowledgements

My gratitude is given to all the wonderful people who touched my life during this journey. Thank you to each of these amazing people who supported me to believe in myself and my journey. To the dearest of people who have played a vital part in shaping myself and my life. There are many incredible people whose hearts and souls touched mine; I know I have had the honour of touching theirs' to. The names are not mentioned here, because I wish to ensure their privacy is kept sacred.

I am constantly inspired by the heart of the human spirit; it comes to you in the oddest of places.

I would love to share a letter, which was written to me, and touched my heart deeply. It is beautifully written in its rawness. I have kept this letter and other letters I received from people whose hearts and souls touched mine. Upon receiving these letters, it is clear to see how powerful the written word is.

The power of the written word, a letter from a friend.

ACKNOWLEDGEMENTS

Hello my Aussie girl,

Man I have missed you.

To quote something you said in our farmhouse retreat, "People only dream of things like this or watch it in the movies. We are living it." I am so very proud of you, Suzie.

You have always been strong and courageous. A woman with deep convictions and character. Willing to follow her heart no matter where it would lead, knowing full well that all will be provided for. Do not lose that vision!!!!!!!!!!!

Your adventure must truly be amazing and I hang on your every word that you write. I wish I could have travelled with you as you are a special woman on a special journey in life. The universe gives us all that we need. Even people, places and things that may feel to us as negative or disheartening serve to provide for us. They strengthen us in areas of weakness and help prepare us as our journey continues. I am sure, that feelings of abandonment and loneliness seek to overcome your joy, but you are being straightened by these things. You have not reached your final destination as yet, for it will be magnificent.

My life is unfolding and my woodworking and vanishing are becoming popular. People want me—yes, at fifty, people love me and want me. They will want you, too. Age is irrelevant. When voices say, "You can't because you are too old", do not receive that.

Look to the universe to make your path and provide all that is designed for you.

I miss you and want you to know that you can lean upon me whenever you need to. I love you and care about you. Now go on your journey with strength.

I had recently met this person; we barely knew each other on one level, yet in this letter it is clear this person knows me well.

I am learning when you courageously follow the guidance of your heart, some strangers see this and warm to you quickly; at times it is quite surreal. Living my life as an adventure has shown me I am not alone on this journey.

Stepping out into the world connects you to people who appear as angels and messengers. From my experience, everyone teaches you something of value, the more you trust, the more this happens.

The world is your playground, go out there and enjoy the adventure of being alive.

www.ingramcontent.com/pod-product-compliance
Lightning Source LLC
Chambersburg PA
CBHW050605300426
44112CB00013B/2080

Thank You!

Can You Help?

As a special bonus for my readers, you can find the full-resolution photos to view at:
https://www.suehelenrobson.com/traveltoliveimages

Did you enjoy this book? Discover something about yourself?

If you like (or don't like) what you have read, I'd love it if you left your HONEST review on the marketplace you purchased this book from.

Reviews are really important to the success of a book.

I really appreciate it.

This will help more people find this book. With this in mind, the more we share our stories, the more people we can help.

Love and Light,

These days I am home now with friends and family. However, this is something I have always loved to do—hey, I still do.

This was not as easy living on board a Super Yacht, so it was vital I found a lounge bar that had a similar feel. During my travels, there were times I was on my own. I had no problem with going to a bar, taking a scrapbook, coloured pencils and finding a pretty place to sit. I enjoyed Margaritas and Daiquiris, and from where I was located most often they were on special. After all the Caribbean, Mexico, and the Bahamas were places I hung out.

Sipping on a Margarita in the comfort of a hammock was all I needed to feel at home. Getting out to order another drink and get back in the hammock, at times was a challenge—hehehe, never mind. it made for some fun banter with those sharing the same space. Needless to say, I have met some amazing people. Turns out not taking yourself seriously while you struggle somewhat awkwardly to get out of the hammock does indeed bring laughter to those around you. . .

I invite you to ponder your dreams, what does that look like for you and how can this best serve others.

I believe everyone has a story of value and meaning. You may be surprised how many people you could help on their journey.

You can find out about how Sue can help you more via her website:

www.suehelenrobson.com

About the Author

Sue is a creative person with a gypsy soul, who is passionate about making a difference in the world.

So, when a series of unexpected events occurred in her early teenage years, it got Sue to question what is life all about, really?

At this time, she made a commitment to herself to live life as an adventure and let the gypsy in her roam freely in many directions.

Sue's quest, in search of the Ultimate Vocation, has taken her on the adventure of a lifetime.

* * *

In my Heart and Soul, I am a laid back lady who enjoys the simple things. After all, I was born in the sixties where peace, love, and mung beans were all the go!

Over the years, I have found a way to create a place that is my feel-good place no matter where I am.

As I am a lover of nourishing food and good wine, from here creating fun is simple. Add some music and a bit of dancing, with candles setting the ambience, good times can be enjoyed. During my travels, this was shared among strangers and new friends. Over time, some of these folks become valuable friends to this day.

A Final Note to the Reader

As we near the end of this book, I want to take a moment to tell you that you don't have to do anything grandeur to make a difference.

Simply just turn up, be your authentic self and show the world who you are.

I encourage you to find your point of difference, for in this lies your unique talents and skills, these are your inner gifts, your medicine that can help you and others on this journey.

And if you are stuck, take a deep breath and ask yourself:

"What is it I want to create?"

Here is an affirmation I enjoy working with; it has supported me during times of change.

"It is safe for me to set inspiring new goals that expand and reinvent my life."

I chose travel as my vehicle, the world as my playground, adventure as my teacher with ambition as my driving force.

I believe you have got this.

Now go on your journey with strength.

Love and Light,
Sue

I look forward to hearing your stories!

You can find out more about how Sue can help you via her website.
www.suehelenrobson.com

Identify & Clarify Mini Career Success Journal

One of the biggest challenges with creating change, be it career path, a lifestyle change or a new direction, is not knowing what to expect or where to start.

Here in this 7-day workbook, I provide you with simple tools to support you to Identify & Clarify what it is you truly want to create.

From this understanding, you can see what may be holding you back, be it self-doubt, fear of the unknown or simply lack of clarity.

If you are ready to discover how you can ignite the fire in your belly and consciously create the changes you seek, you can dive in here by clicking the link below.

I look forward to hearing your stories!

Send me your thoughts and questions.
me@suehelenrobson.com

Love and Light,

Sue

Get access to your 7-day Action Plan at:
https://www.suehelenrobson.com/ttl7dayplan